OWJC
7/12

WHO WAS WILLIAM PENN?

And Other Questions
about the
Founding of Pennsylvania

Marty Rhodes Figley

LERNER PUBLICATIONS COMPANY · MINNEAPOLIS

A Word about Language

English word usage, spelling, grammar, and punctuation have changed over the centuries. We have preserved original spellings and word usage in the quotations included in this book.

Lerner Publications Company
A division of Lerner Publishing Group, Inc.
241 First Avenue North
Minneapolis, MN 55401 U.S.A.

Website address: www.lernerbooks.com

Library of Congress Cataloging-in-Publication Data

Figley, Marty Rhodes, 1948–
    Who was William Penn? : and other questions about the founding of
Pennsylvania / by Marty Rhodes Figley.
    p.   cm. — (Six questions of American history)
    Includes bibliographical references and index.
    ISBN 978–0–7613–5328–7 (lib. bdg. : alk. paper)
    1. Penn, William, 1644–1718—Juvenile literature. 2. Pioneers—Pennsylvania—
Biography—Juvenile literature. 3. Quakers—Pennsylvania—Biography—Juvenile
literature. 4. Pennsylvania—History—Colonial period, ca. 1600–1775—Juvenile
literature. I. Title.
    F152.2.F52 2012
    974.8'02092—dc23 [B]   2011017221

Manufactured in the United States of America
1 – DP – 12/31/11

TABLE OF CONTENTS 4

THE SIX
QUESTIONS
HELP YOU
DISCOVER THE
FACTS!

INTRODUCTION

On the evening of September 3, 1667, a secret meeting took place near the Irish city of Cork. Members of the Society of Friends (a religious group commonly known as Quakers) had gathered to worship. They were breaking the law. If discovered, the Quakers could be thrown in prison—or even tortured.

A tall, handsome young man attended the meeting that night. He didn't look like the others. The Quakers dressed plainly. This young man's fine silk coat was decorated with lace ruffles. But he watched the simple Quaker service with admiration.

Suddenly, a soldier burst through the door! The Quakers didn't believe in violence. So the soldier expected no trouble from them. But the young man rushed toward the soldier and grabbed him. Several Quakers stopped the young man. The soldier was surprised to find this well-dressed gentleman at such a meeting. He turned and fled. But later, he returned with more soldiers.

They arrested the worshippers and herded them into court. The judge saw the finely dressed gentleman and offered to set him free. But the young man refused. His heart was with the Quakers. He would worship with them, defend them, and even go to prison with them. Who was this young man?

Dutch painter Egbert van Heemskerk the Elder (1634–1704) made this artwork of a Quaker meeting. Quakers were among some of the Christian groups who eventually fled Europe for North America. The Quakers had been treated harshly due to their religioius practices.

CURRENT
INTERNATIONAL
BORDER

CITY OR TOWN

COUNTY BORDER

N

SCOTLAND

NORTHERN
IRELAND

NORTH
SEA

IRELAND

IRISH SEA

ENGLAND

NORTH
ATLANTIC
OCEAN

Cork

COUNTY
CORK

WALES

Oxford

Wanstead

Ruscombe

London

ENGLISH CHANNEL

Paris

FRANCE

5

This painting shows London, England, and the Thames River in the mid-1600s, when William Penn lived there.

ONE BECOMING A MAN

The young man's name was William Penn. He was born on October 14, 1644, in London, England. Times were troubled. A civil war had started two years before William was born. King Charles I and his Royalist followers fought against the army of Oliver Cromwell and Parliament. The king believed that God gave him complete power to rule the people. Cromwell and Parliament were representatives elected by the people. They believed that laws Parliament had approved limited the king's power.

a person who supports the king or the queen

a group of lords and elected officials who help govern a country

William's father, also named William, was a talented officer in the British navy. He supported the king. But he also believed in protecting his country from outside attacks, no matter who was in power. In 1644 Oliver Cromwell's army gained control of the British navy. Captain Penn served him well. Cromwell promoted him to vice admiral.

Admiral Penn spent much of his time at sea. William's mother, Margaret, took care of him. Seventeenth-century London was crowded and dirty. When William was three, he survived the deadly disease smallpox.

a contagious, often deadly disease that is caused by the poxvirus

William's father, Admiral William Penn, served in the Britsh navy.

Not long after William's recovery, Admiral Penn came home on leave. He decided to move his family 10 miles (16 kilometers) away from London. William spent much of his early childhood in the country at a house in Wanstead. William loved living close to nature.

The English Civil War ended in 1649. Oliver Cromwell won. Parliament made him ruler. Cromwell's powers were in many ways like those of an uncrowned king. Charles was tried in court, found guilty of treason, and executed. His son, Charles II, escaped to Holland.

In 1652 Cromwell rewarded Admiral Penn for his naval victories. He gave the admiral land near Cork, Ireland, including Macroom Castle. But the family chose to stay in England for the time being.

Oliver Cromwell

William Penn went to Chigwell Free School in Wanstead. The school was founded in about 1629 and still educates about 730 students per year.

William started his formal education at Chigwell Free School. He walked from Wanstead 4 miles (6 km) to and from the school six days a week. William was a good student. By the age of eleven, he could speak and write Latin. William had his first religious experience at Chigwell. He was alone when an inner peace came over him. William believed he felt God communicating directly with him. He remembered this experience for the rest of his life.

the main language of school, church, and state in western Europe until the 1900s

Here is a modern-day photograph of the Tower of London, where Penn's father was imprisoned for five weeks. Prisoners who were accused of crimes against England were kept here. Many prisoners who served sentences were tortured and sent to their deaths.

Meanwhile, Cromwell began to suspect that Admiral Penn was staying in touch with Royalist supporters. Cromwell was furious. He ordered the admiral to be sent to the Tower of London. He further ordered Admiral Penn to retire from the navy.

Tower of London an ancient fortress in London used as a prison during Penn's time

William witnessed his father's humiliation. He saw that power, rank, and importance could be taken away from a person in a moment's time.

After Admiral Penn's release in 1656, he moved the family to Macroom Castle. The farther away he was from Cromwell, the safer he would be. The admiral was at home instead of at sea for a change. He probably taught his athletic son how to hunt, fight with a sword, and shoot a musket. William continued his studies at home with a tutor.

When William was thirteen, his father did something unusual. Admiral Penn was a member of the Church of England. But he invited a Quaker preacher named Thomas Loe to the castle. The family and servants from the castle gathered to hear Loe. He spoke about the Quaker belief that there's an inner light in each person. Perhaps William felt a connection with the Quaker preacher after his religious experience at Chigwell.

Parts of Macroom Castle still stand in County Cork, Ireland. Admiral Penn took his family here after his release from prison.

William began exploring his own religious beliefs. He read his Bible and marked important passages. But William didn't feel he could ask his family questions about the best way to worship God. They didn't worry much about spiritual matters. William felt, "I was a child alone."

The fortunes of the Penn family changed when Cromwell died in 1658. William's father was on the ship that brought Charles II, the restored British king, back to England to reclaim the throne. Afterward, the king made him a knight, and he was known as Sir William Penn.

William's father decided that his son should be well educated. In 1660 William became a student at Oxford University. The famous place of learning had many rules, including daily chapel and a dress code.

During his second year, he attended lectures at the home of Dr. John Owen. Owen preached independent thinking. As a result, William began to question why things were done the way they were at Oxford.

WHAT DID WILLIAM REBEL AGAINST AT OXFORD?

Officially, the Church of England was the only religion in Britain. Students at Oxford were required to attend chapel services. They had to wear surplices (long white gowns with wide sleeves) for religious services. But William searched for his own answers to how he wanted to worship. He refused to attend chapel services or wear the surplice. As a result, he was expelled from Oxford.

English artist David Loggan (1634–1692), made this print of Oxford University. William was sent to further his education at this famous university, but he was expelled for disobeying the rules.

He rebelled against the school's strict religious rules. He was soon expelled.

William's actions disappointed Sir William. He sent William to France where he hoped his son would learn the ways of the French royal court. William enjoyed his time at court, but it didn't hold his interest as religion did. He left Paris and spent time at the Academy of Saumur, a school in western France. William studied with Moses Amyraut. He was a famous Protestant professor who taught freedom of religion and tolerance.

accepting beliefs or practices that differ from one's own

13

WHY WAS WILLIAM WEARING ARMOR?

This portrait of William was painted in 1666 when he was twenty-two. He was thinking of becoming a soldier. On a trip back to Ireland, an uprising occurred at a nearby military post. William fought bravely as a "volunteer soldier" to help end the uprising. The commander of the volunteers, the Duke of Ormonde, praised his skill. He wrote William's father, suggesting that William become a professional soldier. His father didn't think that was a good idea. He warned William not to yield to "his youthful desire."

William returned to England in August 1664 in style. A neighbor described William as having turned into "a most modish [fashionable] person, a fine gentleman." But despite his elegant clothes, William was still searching for answers to questions he had about how to live his life.

In February 1665, William started law school at the Inns of Court in London. When the Great Plague overwhelmed the city that summer, the school closed. William witnessed the Quakers' kindness and bravery as thousands of people died. They helped the sick when no one else would.

a deadly, contagious disease from 1665–1666 that killed one hundred thousand people in London; also called the bubonic plague

In 1666 King Charles II returned Macroom Castle to its original owner. He gave William's father a larger estate and Shangarry Castle outside the city of Cork in Ireland. That fall William traveled to Ireland to manage his father's estate.

One summer day in 1667, William decided to visit a clothing shop in Cork. A Quaker woman owned it. He learned from her that Thomas Loe was to preach that night. William eagerly attended the meeting. When he heard Loe preach again, William felt faint. He later wrote, "It was at this time that the Lord visited me with a certain sound and testimony of His eternal word." William knew he had become a Quaker. The meeting had serious consequences. William, along with other Quakers, was arrested.

> "It was at this time that the Lord visited me with a certain sound and testimony of His eternal word."
> —William Penn

NEXT QUESTION

HOW COULD WILLIAM PENN HELP THE QUAKERS?

William's father *(seated)* asks William *(standing right)* to leave Wanstead for good after learning of his son's wish to become a Quaker. Howard Pyle (1853–1911) illustrates the scene with two women crying, but they were most likely not there.

ᴛᴡᴏ PREACHER, WRITER, FIGHTER

After the Quaker meeting in Cork, William went to prison for the first time. When he was released, his father demanded that he come home at once. It disappointed Sir William that his accomplished son would not choose the career of courtier. Instead, William wanted to throw it all away to be a Quaker!

an attendant at a king's court

William brought a Quaker friend home with him. Perhaps he thought this would protect him from an argument with his father. It didn't. Sir William took his son to a private room in a tavern to talk. He absolutely did not want William to be a Quaker. William knew he would never change his mind. The father and the son couldn't agree. William's father eventually told him to pack his clothes and leave Wanstead.

William was in many ways like his father. Sir William was a skilled warrior who had won countless naval battles. William was a fearless fighter too. After leaving home, he used his law school training, his talent for writing and speaking, and his father's royal connections to fight for the Quakers. He debated in public, protested against religious persecution, and wrote religious pamphlets and tracts.

short written works

William's tract *The Sandy Foundation Shaken* questioned some basic beliefs of the Church of England. On December 12, 1668, the bishop of London ordered William's arrest. William was imprisoned in the Tower of London. The bishop offered William a chance to recant. "My prison shall be my grave before I will budge a jot," was William's answer.

to publicly withdraw a previous statement or belief

His father visited him and unsuccessfully tried to help. King Charles II sent his chaplain to question William. William wrote another tract explaining that he didn't mean to attack the beliefs of the Church of England or the king. Satisfied, King Charles signed an order for his release on July 28, 1669.

William traveled to Ireland and helped free imprisoned Quakers there. After his return to England, he went to prison again for his Quaker activities. But William was still able to be by his father's side when he died September 16, 1670. William arranged an impressive funeral for his father, who was considered a naval hero.

William Penn *(standing in blue coat)* appears in a court of law, where he was sentenced to prison in the Tower of London.

Before his death, Sir William did one last thing for his son. He wrote the king and the king's brother, the Duke of York, asking them to continue their favor toward his son. But even the king couldn't totally protect William when he broke the law. In 1671 William went to prison for refusing to take an oath not to take up arms against the king. William asked why that was necessary since Quakers believe in nonviolence toward all people. He was released from prison after six months.

The next year, on April 4, 1672, William married Gulielma Maria Springett, a lovely Quaker girl he admired. He thought of her as the "joy of his life."

In 1675 two Quakers who owned land in western New Jersey, a British colony, asked William to settle a dispute between them. Because of his legal experience and skill, he was successful. He then helped draft a plan of government for the colony. He called the plan *Concessions and Agreements*. It provided religious freedom for all and "put the power in the people."

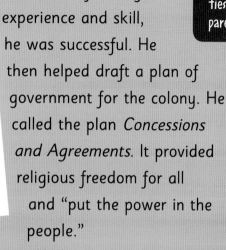

a group of people living in a new territory but maintaining ties with the parent state

WHERE IS EUROPE?
The continent of Europe lies across the North Sea and the English Channel from the modern-day United Kingdom. In the 1600s, this country was made up of England, Ireland, Scotland, and Wales.

William tirelessly continued his work for the Quakers. He traveled to Holland, Germany, and Ireland to tell others about the Quaker faith. He fought to change the laws that punished the Quakers.

Some Quakers had already left Europe to avoid persecution. They had settled in the New Jersey colony. But William dreamed of a new colony large enough to provide a home for thousands of Quakers.

The king's brother owned a vast amount of land on the western side of the Delaware River. (Some of this land would later become the state of Delaware.) William remembered that, many years before, his father had loaned King Charles a huge sum of money. William took a bold step. He wrote to the king asking for the duke's land as payment for the debt.

King Charles II knew that giving William the land would solve several problems. He could pay off the debt owed to Penn, encourage colonial trade, and provide a way to get the troublesome Quakers out of the country. The king would appear to be religiously tolerant to his opponents by granting this land to a Quaker. On March 4, 1681, the king agreed to William's request. William Penn was now the sole proprietor of 46,000 square miles (119,000 sq. km) of land in

someone granted ownership of a colony and power to govern and distribute its land

King Charles II gives William Penn (right in black hat and coat) the charter (written contract) for land in what would come to be called Pennsylvania. Allan Stewart (1865–1951) painted this scene. The charter was payment for a debt owed by King Charles II to Admiral Penn.

LAWS AGAINST QUAKERS

Many English laws targeted Quakers. It was illegal for five or more Quakers to meet. Practicing any religion other than the Church of England was illegal. Quakers refused to take oaths. But people who did not take an oath of loyalty to the king could hold no secret meetings. Such people were often charged with contempt of court. Quakers were fined, imprisoned, tortured, and sold into slavery as a result of their religious beliefs.

British North America. King Charles II chose the name Pennsylvania for the new colony in honor of William's father. The word *sylvan* means "forest land" in Latin.

William hoped Pennsylvania would be an example to other nations, a "holy experiment." Everyone would have the freedom to follow their religious beliefs without fear of punishment.

NEXT QUESTION

 **WHAT** WOULD WILLIAM PENN HAVE TO DO TO CREATE HIS "HOLY EXPERIMENT"?

This illustration shows Native Americans of the Delaware River valley trading with Swedish settlers, who occupied the region before the arrival of William Penn.

THREE "AN EXAMPLE TO THE NATIONS"

William worked energetically to plan his new colony. He had acquired the land. Some Dutch and Swedish settlers lived in the area. But he still needed to convince more people to move there. Because of his travels, he had many contacts in Germany, Holland, and France. He wrote them about his grant, encouraging them to move to Pennsylvania.

William also published tracts about the advantages of living in Pennsylvania. He encouraged first adventurers who were hardworking, skilled craftsmen to consider the move. He did not mention religion in these tracts. He wanted to

Pennsylvania's first settlers

reach a larger group, not just Quakers. William offered land for sale at a good price. Landholders would be required to pay him a small quitrent.

a fixed rent

In April 1681, William appointed his cousin William Markham to serve as Pennsylvania's deputy governor until he could travel there himself. Markham arrived in early summer. William instructed the deputy governor to establish good relationships with the European settlers and the Native Americans who already lived there. He told Markham "to be tender of offending the Indians." William sent letters to both groups, assuring them of his good intentions. Markham was also supposed to find the best site for a port city along the Delaware River. William chose the name Philadelphia for this city.

a city located on a coast or shore where many ships can dock

PHILADELPHIA

The name *Philadelphia* means "brotherly love." The name comes from the Greek words *philos* (love) and *adelphos* (brother). William became the first city planner in British North America when he designed this "green country town." He wanted it to be different from the crowded, unhealthy cities in Europe. He dreamed of a place "which will never be burnt, and always be wholesome." Streets were straight and wide. Each plot of land had room for "gardens and orchards and fields." The city's population grew to twenty-five thousand people within its first two years.

Writing the laws to govern his new colony was William's most challenging job. After years of suffering under English laws, he wanted to make Pennsylvania's government an example of justice and freedom for all nations. During March 1681, he began to work on the new constitution. As he formed his ideas, William sought the opinion of men whom he admired. He completed the Frame of Government of Pennsylvania during the spring of 1682. He organized the government into three parts. The Council was to make the

a set of basic principles and laws

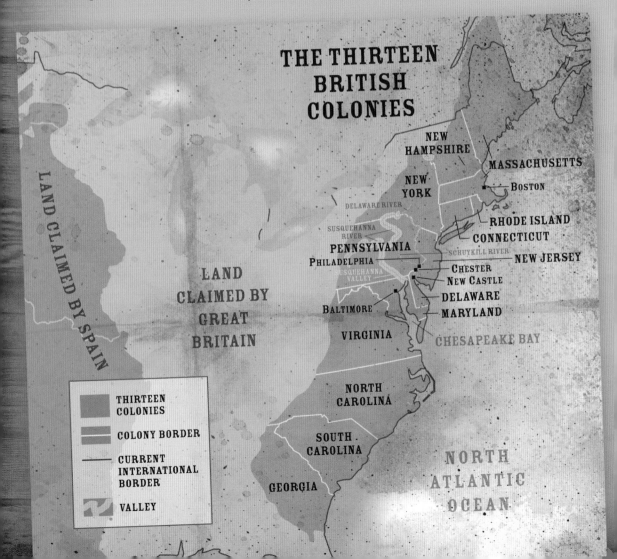

THE THIRTEEN BRITISH COLONIES

LAND CLAIMED BY SPAIN

LAND CLAIMED BY GREAT BRITAIN

NEW HAMPSHIRE

MASSACHUSETTS

BOSTON

NEW YORK

DELAWARE RIVER

SUSQUEHANNA RIVER

PENNSYLVANIA

PHILADELPHIA

SUSQUEHANNA VALLEY

SCHUYKILL RIVER

RHODE ISLAND

CONNECTICUT

NEW JERSEY

CHESTER

NEW CASTLE

DELAWARE

MARYLAND

BALTIMORE

VIRGINIA

CHESAPEAKE BAY

NORTH CAROLINA

SOUTH CAROLINA

GEORGIA

NORTH ATLANTIC OCEAN

THIRTEEN COLONIES

COLONY BORDER

CURRENT INTERNATIONAL BORDER

VALLEY

William Penn's First Frame of Government of Pennsylvania was written in April 1682.

laws. The General Assembly would vote on them. These two bodies made up the legislature. A governor (William Penn) with limited powers would direct and manage the colony.

the lawmaking body in a government

As the proprietor of Pennsylvania, William could have given himself the powers of a king, but he chose not to do that. All men who owned property had the right to vote. They elected the members of the Council and the General Assembly. Amendments (changes) could be made to the constitution if seven-eighths of the legislature and the governor approved them. This constitution was the first one to allow amendments. The constitution protected many individual rights, including freedom of religion, freedom of the press, and trial by jury. (This right also applied to Native Americans.) The death penalty was only applied to murder. No taxation could take place without the approval of the voters.

After a year of preparation, William was finally ready to travel to his new colony. His wife was expecting their fourth child. She and the children planned to join him later. On August 30, 1682, William boarded the ship *Welcome* with other adventurers and set sail for Pennsylvania.

The voyage took two months. Sailing across the ocean at that time was often unpleasant. Passengers were crowded into cramped quarters. They could not bathe and were often seasick. During the trip, an outbreak of smallpox killed thirty-one passengers. Because William had had the disease as a child, he was immune to it. Since he couldn't catch it again, he was able to help care for the sick.

The *Welcome* reached New Castle, Delaware, on the night of October 27, 1682. The next day, William met with officials, including William Markham. Then he sailed up the

In this print, made in 1882, William Penn arrives on the shores of New Castle, Delaware. He is met by other colonists and American Indians.

U.S. artist Benjamin West (1738–1820) painted this scene of William Penn talking with the American Indians in Pennsylvania in 1682. He made the Great Treaty with them. No land could be taken away from them. He hoped for peaceful relations with the native peoples.

Delaware River to see the site for Philadelphia. About 25 miles (40 km) farther up the river, Penn inspected the place where he would build his family home, Pennsbury Manor.

Soon after his arrival, he began talks with the Native Americans. Many European settlers had viewed them as savages who had no rights. William was determined to treat the Native Americans with fairness and dignity. He visited their villages, ate their food, learned their language, and even ran foot races with them.

Under "English law," William's charter gave him ownership of all the land in Pennsylvania. But he insisted that no land be taken from the Native Americans except by purchase. William hoped the purchase of Indian land would also help end boundary disputes.

WHAT WAS THE BOUNDARY DISPUTE ABOUT?

Because of faulty maps and bad surveying, the Pennsylvania charter boundaries differed from those set in the Maryland charter (issued in 1632). Maryland's northern border cut through what William Penn claimed as the city of Philadelphia. According to the Maryland charter, the city no longer was located at the meeting point of the Delaware and Schuylkill rivers. If Philadelphia was to be a successful port city, it needed to be located on waterways that oceangoing ships could reach. According to Pennsylvania's charter, the colony's southern border extended inland, below the head of Maryland's Chesapeake Bay. Both Lord Baltimore and William Penn thought their versions of the borders were the correct ones.

Lord Baltimore was the proprietor of Maryland. He disagreed with the boundaries set by William's Pennsylvania charter. William further angered Lord Baltimore by writing Maryland planters along what he thought was his border, telling them they no longer had to pay taxes to Maryland. The men met several times but could not reach an understanding. After two years, the boundary dispute had gotten worse. Lord Baltimore sailed to

England to argue his case before the king's Privy Council.

a group of people who are appointed to advise the king on political affairs

William knew he needed to do the same. He set sail on August 12, 1684.

But William felt sadness as he sailed away from his new home. In his farewell letter to Pennsylvania, he wrote, "My love & my life is to you & with you, & no waters can quench it nor distance were [wear] it out or bring it to an end."

Pennsylvania had grown much since its founding. In three years, more than seven thousand people from England, Wales, Ireland, Holland, Sweden, and Germany had settled in the colony. Trade was booming. William's Frame of Government (with some revisions made by the legislature) had been put in place. Indeed, the new colony was blossoming.

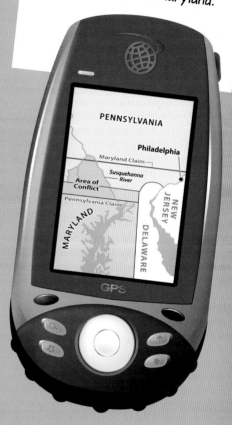

PENNSYLVANIA/MARYLAND BOUNDARY DISPUTE
This map shows the area of boundary disputes between Pennsylvania and Maryland.

NEXT QUESTION

WHEN WOULD WILLIAM RETURN TO PENNSYLVANIA?

King James II and his wife Queen Mary *(both seated in front)* attend their coronation in 1685.

FOUR TIMES OF TROUBLE AND TRIUMPH

William's ship arrived in England on October 6, 1684. It docked only "seven miles [11 km] from my own home," he later wrote. After two long years, William was reunited with his wife and children.

But he soon discovered that his assistant, Philip Lemain, had not packed important papers. William needed them for his argument about the boundary dispute. He sent an exasperated letter back to Pennsylvania, demanding that the papers be sent immediately. "I am now here with my finger in my mouth," he wrote.

King Charles II was preoccupied with matters other than boundaries, however. Parliament was challenging the king's power. Charles responded by cracking down on all political and religious troublemakers, including the Quakers. His tyranny soon ended. Four months after William's return, Charles II had a stroke and died.

In February 1685, the Duke of York, Charles's brother, was crowned King James II. James was a Catholic. Parliament was filled with Protestants. As a result, he was an unpopular ruler. But he had been a friend of Admiral Penn and William for many years. In late 1685, the new king settled the boundary dispute in William's favor. Probably because of William's influence, James II pardoned of all religious prisoners in March 1686. More than thirteen hundred Quakers were released from prison.

The king's actions stirred up fear that he would replace the Church of England with the Catholic Church. Protestant leaders looked for an alternative to James. They found it in William of Orange, the Protestant leader of Holland and husband to James's daughter Mary.

William of Orange

King James II flees to France after William of Orange arrives in Britain. British artist Andrew Carrick Gow (1848–1920) painted this scene in 1888.

Parliament asked William of Orange to take over the throne. He arrived on Britain's shores with fourteen thousand troops. James's army deserted him, and he escaped to France. The new king, William III, was crowned on April 11, 1689.

Since William Penn had been close friends with King James II, he was branded a traitor. William went into hiding. He spent money he didn't have just to live. He had used much of his fortune to fund Pennsylvania. He didn't manage his finances well. Colonists in Pennsylvania resented paying their quitrent to an absent landlord, so they didn't. William had trusted his steward Philip Ford to manage his finances. But Ford claimed that William owed him a large sum of money.

In spring 1692, William lost his proprietorship of Pennsylvania. King William III appointed a royal governor

a person who manages the finances and property of another

who wasn't a Quaker to take William's place. In 1693 some of William's friends at court convinced the king to clear William of all charges. William then worked hard to regain control over Pennsylvania. Finally, King William III gave him a new charter.

The new charter required William to return to Pennsylvania and govern the colony personally. He had to agree to supply the king with troops in Pennsylvania. Fighting wars was against William's beliefs, but to regain his proprietorship, he agreed. The king had the power to force colonists to provide soldiers, no matter who was proprietor of Pennsylvania.

Sorrow continued to haunt William. On February 23, 1694, his beloved wife, Guli, died. She would never see Pennsylvania. And William didn't have enough money to travel to Pennsylvania. Until he could get his finances in order, he once again appointed William Markham as deputy governor.

Five years later, on September 3, 1699, William boarded the *Canterbury* and sailed to Pennsylvania. Traveling with him was Lititia, his youngest daughter from his first marriage, and his new wife, Hannah, who was expecting their first child.

Before the ship sailed, William sent a loving letter to the Quakers in Europe. In it he wrote, "I must leave you but I can never forget you."

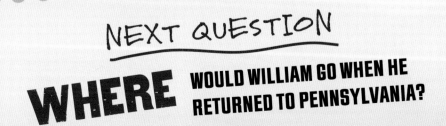

NEXT QUESTION

WHERE WOULD WILLIAM GO WHEN HE RETURNED TO PENNSYLVANIA?

Here is a bird's-eye view of Philadelphia made in 1702, soon after William returned to Pennsylvania.

FIVE RETURN TO AMERICA

The winter voyage took longer than usual. William and his family arrived in Chester, Pennsylvania, on December 1, 1699. William Penn had become a legend. An admiring crowd of settlers and Native Americans gathered on the banks of the Delaware River to greet them.

The next day, William visited the city of brotherly love. He must have been pleased. Philadelphia, with a population of twenty-five thousand, was second only to Boston as the largest city in America. It was a bustling shipping center. Along the tree-lined streets stood hundreds of handsome brick houses along with shops, churches, and schools.

In 1700 a pastor in the city wrote, "If anyone were to see Philadelphia who had not been there, he would be astonished beyond measure that it was founded less than twenty years ago."

William had much business to attend to. For years pirates had sailed along the colony's coastlines robbing other ships and terrorizing people. Some colonists illegally engaged in smuggling. William called a meeting of the legislature and condemned smuggling and piracy.

> "If anyone were to see Philadelphia who had not been there, he would be astonished beyond measure that it was founded less than twenty years ago."
> — Philadelphia pastor

He negotiated a treaty with Native Americans for land in the Susquehanna Valley and in central Pennsylvania. He once again made a point of showing respect by visiting the Native Americans in their homes. Their trust in him was so great that he became a mediator of wars between the tribes.

mediator: someone who helps two sides reach an agreement

In April 1701, William met with the governors of New York and Virginia. They discussed a plan to improve relations and trade among the colonies. William proposed that the colonies unite with a common currency, streamlined court procedures, and mutual cooperation to fight crime. The king and most of the colonists largely ignored the plan. They didn't understand its importance. William's ideas were ahead of their time.

In Philadelphia Quakers were able to mingle freely and walk the streets without fear after a Quaker meeting.

The squabbling among the members of the Pennsylvania Assembly and Council saddened William. They were dissatisfied with the old Frame of Government. But they couldn't agree on a new one. William urged the politicians to "study peace and be at unity. Provide for the good of all."

Then news came from Britain that politicians wanted to turn all individually owned colonies into royal provinces. William knew he had to return to Britain to personally protect his colony.

a colony where the king has complete control over its government

A few days before William left for Britain, the legislature finally approved a new Frame of Government of Pennsylvania. The biggest change was a shift in power from the Council to the General Assembly. The new legislation gave more power

This farm provided a stop along the road from Pennsbury Manor.

to the elected officials and less to William, the proprietor. The new laws, called the Charter of Privileges, still protected religious freedom for all.

In early November 1701, William and his family left Pennsbury Manor. They sailed away from Pennsylvania.

NEXT QUESTION

WHY DID WILLIAM NEVER RETURN TO HIS BELOVED PENNSYLVANIA?

This is a print of William Penn's Philadelphia home. It was published in *Cassell's History of the United States*, volume 1, by Edmund Ollier, printed in the 1870s.

SIX SORROW AND SUCCESS

The Penn family arrived in Britain on December 31, 1701. King William III died a few months later, on March 8, 1702. (His wife, Mary, had died in 1694.) His sister-in-law, James II's other daughter, was crowned Queen Anne. William used all his diplomatic skills to win favor with the new queen. When William and a group of Quakers visited her at court, she told him, "You and your friends may be assured of my protection."

   The last years of William's life were weighed down by more money problems. Establishing Pennsylvania had cost him dearly. He had difficulty collecting the quitrents from the colonists. No one in Pennsylvania seemed to remember the sacrifices he had made. In a letter to his friend James Logan, William wrote, "O, Pennsylvania! What hast thou cost me?"

To make matters worse, after Philip Ford died, Ford's relatives took William to court. They insisted that he owed them money. On January 7, 1708, at the age of sixty-three, William went to debtors' prison. He stayed there for nine months. Finally, Quaker friends helped pay his debt.

a prison for people unable to pay their debts

Even during this difficult time, William still dreamed of going back to Pennsylvania. He wrote to Logan on May 3, 1708, "I hope next spring, if not next fall, to set forth." But he never saw Pennsylvania again.

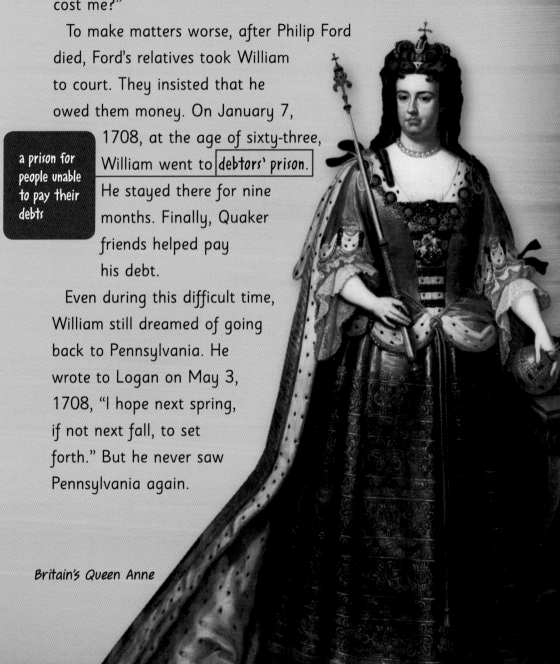

Britain's Queen Anne

William moved back to England and lived in Ruscombe.

William settled his family in a large home in Ruscombe, England. Despite his poor health, he continued his work for the Quakers. William suffered several strokes during the last seven years of his life. He died on July 30, 1718. But William's family members continued to hold the proprietorship to Pennsylvania until the Revolutionary War (1775–1783). Then it became one of the first thirteen states.

From his own life experiences, William knew what could happen without religious freedom. A person who chose to worship in a different way could be persecuted, imprisoned, or even killed. Throughout his life, William stood up for what he believed, no matter what the cost. A place that allowed freedom of worship for all was his cherished dream.

This statue of William Penn tops Philadelphia City Hall, which was completed in 1901.

William's "holy experiment" achieved much of what he dreamed and more. Immigrants with different religious beliefs— from all parts of Europe— found a welcoming home in Pennsylvania. The constitution William helped create guaranteed individual rights. It provided for checks and balances on government power. Pennsylvania's constitution set an example that influenced the U.S. Constitution and the Bill of Rights. A magnificent 37-foot statue of William on top of Philadelphia's city hall honors his accomplishments. William still watches over his city of brotherly love.

NEXT QUESTION

HOW DO WE KNOW ABOUT WILLIAM PENN AND THE FOUNDING OF PENNSYLVANIA?

Primary Source: Penn's Advertisement for Pennsylvania

The best way to see into the past and learn about any historical event is with primary sources. Primary sources are those created near the time being studied. They include diaries, letters, newspaper articles, documents, speeches, personal papers, pamphlets, photos, paintings, and other items. They are made by people who have direct, firsthand knowledge of the event.

During his lifetime, William Penn produced at least fifty written works. The following is part of a letter that William wrote on August 16, 1683, to convince people to make a new home in Pennsylvania.

The air is sweet and clear, the heavens serene, like the south parts of France, rarely overcast.

The fruits that I find in the woods are the white and black mulberry, chestnut, walnut, plums, strawberries, cranberries, huckleberries, and grapes of divers sorts.

For food as well as profit, the elk, as big as a small ox, deer bigger than ours, beaver, raccoon, rabbits [and] squirrels . . . . Of fowl of the land, there is the turkey (forty and fifty pound weight), . . . pheasants, heath-birds, pigeons, and partridges in abundance.

The woods are adorned with lovely flowers, for color, greatness, figure, and variety. I have seen the gardens of London best stored with that sort of beauty, but think they may be improved by our woods.

WRITE YOUR OWN ADVERTISEMENT FOR A COLONY

You have recently arrived in British North America. You want to convince some of your relatives to come here too. Write a letter telling about all the wonderful things in your colony.

WHO are you?

WHERE did you originally come from?

WHY did you come here?

WHEN did you arrive?

WHAT are the good things about the colony?

WHAT is the weather like?

WHAT are the plants and vegetables like?

WHAT is the wildlife like?

HOW is it better than your old home?

WHY should your relatives come here?

USE **WHO, WHAT, WHERE WHY, WHEN,** AND **HOW** TO THINK OF OTHER QUESTIONS TO HELP YOU CREATE YOUR STORY!

Timeline

1644
William Penn is born in London, England, on October 14.

1656
William and his family move to Ireland.

1657
William hears the Quaker Thomas Loe speak at Macroom Castle.

1660
William attends Oxford University.

1662
William is expelled from Oxford.

1663–1664
William studies in France

1665
William begins to study law.

1667
William hears Quaker Thomas Loe speak again. William becomes a Quaker.

William is arrested for the first time.

1672
William marries Gulielma Springett.

1675
William writes the New Jersey charter.

1681
King Charles II gives William the Royal Charter of Pennsylvania on March 4.

1682
William travels to British North America.

1684
William returns to Britain to settle a boundary dispute with Lord Baltimore, the ruler of Maryland.

1685
King Charles is succeeded by his brother, James II.
James II settles the boundary dispute in William's favor.

1686

James II frees religious prisoners, including more than thirteen hundred Quakers.

1688

Parliament offers the British crown to James' son-in-law, William of Orange.

1689

William of Orange is crowned king of England, Scotland, and Ireland.

William is branded a traitor because of his friendship with King James II.

1691

William goes into hiding.

1692

William loses the Pennsylvania proprietorship.

1693

William is cleared of charges.

1694

Wife Gulielma dies on February 23.

William regains the proprietorship of Pennsylvania.

1696

William marries Hannah Callowhill.

1699

William returns to Pennsylvania.

1701

The legislature adopts Pennsylvania's Charter of Privileges.
William and his family return to Britain.

1705

Philip Ford's relatives sue William for debts.

1708

William goes to debtor's prison.
Quaker friends pay off William's debt.

1718

William Penn dies at his home in Ruscombe, England, on July 30.

1901

A statue of William is put on top of Philadelphia City Hall.

Source Notes

12 William Penn, *The Papers of William Penn* (Philadelphia: University of Pennsylvania Press, 1981–1987), 1:265.

14 Catherine Owens Peare, *William Penn: A Biography* (Ann Arbor: University of Michigan Press, 1966), 46.

14 Penn, *Papers* 1:42.

15 Ibid., 1:477.

15 Ibid.

17 Peare, *William Penn*, 83.

18 Penn, *Papers*, 2:270.

19 Ibid., 1:416.

21 Ibid., 2:108.

23 Ibid., 2:120.

23 Ibid., 2:121.

23 Ibid.

28–29 Ibid., 2:590.

30 Ibid., 2:604.

30 Ibid., 2:601.

30 Ibid., 5:479.

35 Russell Frank Weigley, Nicholas B. Wainwright, Edwin Wolf II, Mary Maples Dunn, Richard Slater Dunn, Edwin B. Bronner, Theodore Thayer, et al. *Philadelphia: A 300-Year History* (New York: W. W. Norton, 1982), 14.

35 Ibid.

36 Samuel Janney, *The Life of William Penn* (Freeport, NY: Books for Libraries Press, 1970), 411.

38 Ibid., 443.

39 Peare, *William Penn*, 394.

39 Ibid., 404.

42 Penn, *Papers*, 2:446.

Selected Bibliography

Dunn, R. S. and M. M. Dunn, eds. *The World of William Penn*. Philadelphia: University of Pennsylvania Press, 1986.

Illick, Joseph. *William Penn the Politician*. Ithaca, NY: Cornell University Press, 1965.

Janney, Samuel. *The Life of William Penn*. Freeport, NY: Books for Libraries Press, 1970.

Peare, Catherine Owens. *William Penn: A Biography*. Ann Arbor: University of Michigan Press, 1966.

Penn, William. *The Papers of William Penn*. Philadelphia: University of Pennsylvania Press, 1981–1987.

Weigley. Russell Frank, Nicholas B. Wainwright, Edwin Wolf II, Mary Maples Dunn, Richard Slater Dunn, Edwin B. Bronner, Theodore Thayer, et al. *Philadelphia: A 300-Year History*. New York: W. W. Norton, 1982.

Further Reading and Websites

Discover Pennsylvania
http://sites.state.pa.us/kids/
This is a great site with everything you could want to know about Pennsylvania, plus kid pages and lots of links.

Kid Info Information on Middle Colonies
http://www.kidinfo.com/american_history/colonization_mid_colonies.html
Become an expert on the history of the middle colonies, including Pennsylvania, by exploring the links on this site.

Levine, Michelle. *The Delaware*. Minneapolis: Lerner Publications Company, 2007. Meet the Delaware Indians, and learn about their history and their customs.

Lutz, Norma Jean. *William Penn Founder of Democracy*. Philadelphia: Chelsea House Publishers, 2000. This is a very well-done biography of William Penn.

Pennsbury Manor
http://www.pennsburymanor.org/
This site is all about William Penn's home in Pennsylvania, Pennsbury Manor.

Swain, Gwenyth. *Freedom Seeker: A Story about William Penn*. Minneapolis: Lerner Publications Company, 2003. Swain offers a nice introduction to the life of William Penn.

———. *Pennsylvania*. Minneapolis: Lerner Publications Company, 2001. This is a colorful, nicely illustrated book full of facts about Pennsylvania.

ushistory.org
http://www.ushistory.org/index.html
This excellent site provides access to many interesting links about Philadelphia and American history.

Walker, Sally M. *Written in Bone*. Minneapolis: Carolrhoda Books, 2009. This award-winning author works with scientists to decipher clues from America's colonial past.

Woog, Adam. *What Makes Me a Quaker?* San Diego: KidHaven Press, 2004. This book explains the Quaker religion in an easily understandable way.

Index

Photo Acknowledgments

The images in this book are used with the permission of: © iStockphoto.com/DNY59, p. 1; © iStockphoto.com/Skip O'Donnell, pp. 1 (background) and all wooden plank backgrounds; © iStockphoto.com/sx70, pp. 3 (top), 12, 14 (left), 21 (top), 23, 28; © iStockphoto.com/Ayse Nazli Deliormanli, pp. 3 (bottom), 43 (bottom left); © iStockphoto.com/Serdar Yagci, pp. 4–5 (background), 43 (background); © Laura Westlund/Independent Picture Service, pp. 4–5 (top), 19 (inset), 24, 29 (inset); © The Bridgeman Art Library/Getty Images, pp. 4–5 (bottom); © Museum of London/The Art Archive/Art Resource, NY, p. 6; © National Maritime Museum, London/The Image Works, p. 7; © Hulton Archive/Getty Images, pp. 8, 39; © North Wind Picture Archives, pp. 9, 18, 36, 44; © iStockphoto.com/Andrey Pustovoy, pp. 10, 25, 41 (top); © JTB Photo/SuperStock, p. 10 (inset); © Joe Fox/Alamy, p. 11; © Eileen Tweedy/The Art Archive/Art Resource, NY, p. 13; Courtesy of the Philadelphia History Museum at the Atwater Kent, The Historical Society of Pennsylvania Collection, p. 14 (right); © Mary Evans Picture Library/The Image Works, p. 16; © iStockphoto.com/Talshiar, pp. 19, 29 (top); © John Noott Galleries, Broadway, Worcestershire, UK/The Bridgeman Art Library, p. 20; The Library Company of Philadelphia, p. 22; Courtesy of the Pennsylvania State Archives, in Basic Documents of Pennsylvania Including Proprietary Charters and Deeds, Indian Deeds, and State Constitutions, 1681–1873, Record Group 26, Records of the Department of State, p. 25 (inset); The Granger Collection, New York, p. 26; © Eileen Tweedy/Parker Gallery London/The Art Archive/Art Resource, NY, p. 27; © Universal Images Group/Hulton Archive/Getty Images, p. 30; © National Maritime Museum, London/The Image Works, p. 31; © Tate Gallery London/The Art Archive/Art Resource, NY, p. 32; © The New York Public Library/Art Resource, NY, p. 34; © SuperStock/SuperStock, p. 37 (top); © Print Collector/HIP/The Image Works, p. 38; © Cotswold Photo Library/Alamy, p. 40; © J. McGrail/ClassicStock/Alamy, p. 41 (inset); Library of Congress, p. 43 (bottom right, LC-USZC4-12141); © PCJones/Alamy, p. 45.

Front cover: Library of Congress (LC-USZC4-12141). Back cover: © iStockphoto.com/Skip O'Donnell.

Main body text set in Sassoon Sans Regular 13.5/20. Typeface provided by Monotype Typography.